THE MORMON TRAIL

A TRUE BOOK®

by

Elaine Landau

Children's Press®
A Division of Scholastic Inc.
New York Toronto London Auckland Sydney
Mexico City New Delhi Hong Kong
Danbury, Connecticut

A statue of Brigham Young (center) honoring the founding of Salt Lake City, Utah

Content Consultant
William G. Hartley
Associate Professor of History
Brigham Young University

Reading Consultant
Dr. Cecilia Minden-Cupp
Former Director, Language
and Literacy Program
Harvard Graduate School
of Education

Author's Dedication
**For Emily, Allison, Ava,
and Julia**

The illustration on the cover shows settlers pulling handcarts across the plains on the Mormon Trail. The photograph on the title page shows wagon tracks that were part of the Mormon and Oregon trails in Wyoming.

Library of Congress Cataloging-in-Publication Data
Landau, Elaine.
   The Mormon Trail / by Elaine Landau.
      p. cm. — (A true book)
   Includes bibliographical references and index.
   ISBN 0-516-25872-9 (lib. bdg.)   0-516-27904-1 (pbk.)
   1. Mormon Pioneer National Historic Trail—History—Juvenile litera-
ture. 2. Mormon Pioneers—West (U.S.)—History—19th century—Juvenile
literature. 3. Frontier and pioneer life—West (U.S.)—Juvenile literature.
4. West (U.S.)—History—19th century—Juvenile literature. 5. Mormon
Church—United States—History—19th century—Juvenile literature.
I. Title. II. Series.
F593.L235 2006
978—dc22   2005003638

CHILDREN'S PRESS, and A TRUE BOOK™, and associated logos are
trademarks and/or registered trademarks of Scholastic Library Publishing.
SCHOLASTIC and associated logos are trademarks and/or registered
trademarks of Scholastic Inc.
1 2 3 4 5 6 7 8 9 10 R 15 14 13 12 11 10 09 08 07 06

Contents

This photograph from about 1847 shows the town of Nauvoo, Illinois.

Time to Leave Nauvoo

It was the fall of 1845, and some people in Nauvoo, Illinois, were anxious. They knew they would soon have to leave their homes and head west. While others had gone west to find gold or to tame a wild frontier, these people were leaving because they weren't safe.

They were members of The Church of Jesus Christ of Latter-day Saints. They were also known as Mormons.

A man named Joseph Smith had established this religion on April 6, 1830. Many saw Smith as a **prophet,** or a person who spoke for God. Over the years, church membership greatly increased.

Life had never been easy for the Mormons, however. Although most were hardworking and

Religious founder Joseph Smith (right) preaches to his Mormon followers (below).

After storming the jail holding Joseph Smith and his brother, a mob of townspeople killed the two men.

honest, their neighbors didn't like or trust them. Many people in Nauvoo disagreed with some of the Mormon beliefs. They were fearful of the new religion and its growing power in the community.

At times, angry **mobs** attacked Mormons and burned their homes. Joseph Smith and his brother, Hyrum, were jailed and later killed by a mob on June 27, 1844. The Mormons knew they had to get out of Nauvoo and find a safe place to live. It wasn't the first time they were forced to leave an area.

Brigham Young, another Mormon leader in Illinois, took charge after Joseph Smith's death. A year later, hoping to calm things down, Young promised the town that 15,000 Mormons would leave the Nauvoo area by spring. But Young thought mobs or even lawmakers

Brigham Young was an important Mormon leader.

might strike again so he
asked some of his followers
to leave before spring.

The Mormons needed a
place to practice their religion
without fear. Young hoped
to find such a place in a
region that Joseph Smith
had spoken about before
his death. Young would lead
the Mormons to a spot deep
within the Rocky Mountains
where they could rebuild
their lives.

Before his death, Joseph Smith said he had a vision of Mormons traveling to the Rocky Mountains.

A map of the trail that the
Mormons followed in 1846–1847

To reach their **promised land,** the **Mormon pioneers** had to travel nearly 1,300 miles (2,092 kilometers). They passed through what are now the states of Iowa, Nebraska, and Wyoming. They took a route that became known as the Mormon Trail. The Mormons hoped to find peace and happiness at the trail's end. But first, they had to survive the trip. It was a trip that tested their faith and unity as a people.

On the Road

The first group of Mormons left Nauvoo, Illinois, on February 4, 1846. Many of the others followed in the later months. They left behind homes, farms, shops, businesses, and many of their belongings.

One family traded their house and a large farm for a

The Mormons left Nauvoo, Illinois, to travel west in 1846.

pair of oxen. Most of their
neighbors had refused to buy
the family's property. Townspeople knew that after the

Mormons had been driven out, they could seize whatever they wanted.

Traveling west in the winter was difficult, but this first group of Mormons felt they had no choice. After they crossed the Mississippi River into Iowa, the weather turned worse. These men, women, and children faced freezing temperatures and snow, then sleet, rain, and mud. Some days, they advanced only

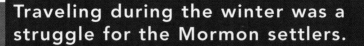

Traveling during the winter was a struggle for the Mormon settlers.

about a 1/2 mile (less than 1 km) in the covered wagons they had built themselves.

Brigham Young hoped to reach the Rocky Mountains by fall. He soon realized that it wasn't possible to get there without stopping along the way. So, after arriving in Iowa, Young ordered groups of his followers to set up temporary camps as they traveled.

People in these camps rested and prepared for the big groups coming later. They built cabins, marked roads, dug wells, and put up fences

On the way to Utah, Mormon pioneers set up camps in Iowa.

The early Mormon settlers built ferries to carry their people and wagons across the rivers.

to protect their cattle. Workers also plowed the ground and planted crops. They built **ferries** and bridges at river crossings. The idea was to make the journey easier for the large Mormon groups that would follow.

Some Mormon pioneers hired themselves out to do odd jobs as they traveled. Some split rails, shucked corn,

The temporary Mormon camps were communities full of activity.

Along parts of the Mormon Trail, some pioneers worked at odd jobs, such as building cabins, to earn money.

and helped build cabins and brick buildings in communities along the way. Women offered dishes, bedding, pots, and pans in exchange for corn, bacon, and cattle feed.

The Nauvoo Brass Band even gave concerts. With their earnings, the Mormon pioneers bought additional supplies for the journey.

As expected, stopping to build the camps slowed the Mormons' journey. It took months for them to reach the Missouri River on the other side of Iowa. At that point, they had traveled about 265 miles (426 km). Across the river lay Nebraska and the start of the second part of their journey.

Moving On

The Mormon pioneers crossed the Missouri River to reach Nebraska, where they set up new camps. In October 1846, near today's Omaha, Nebraska, they established a camp called Winter Quarters. By then, many thousands more had left Nauvoo and crossed Iowa to join them.

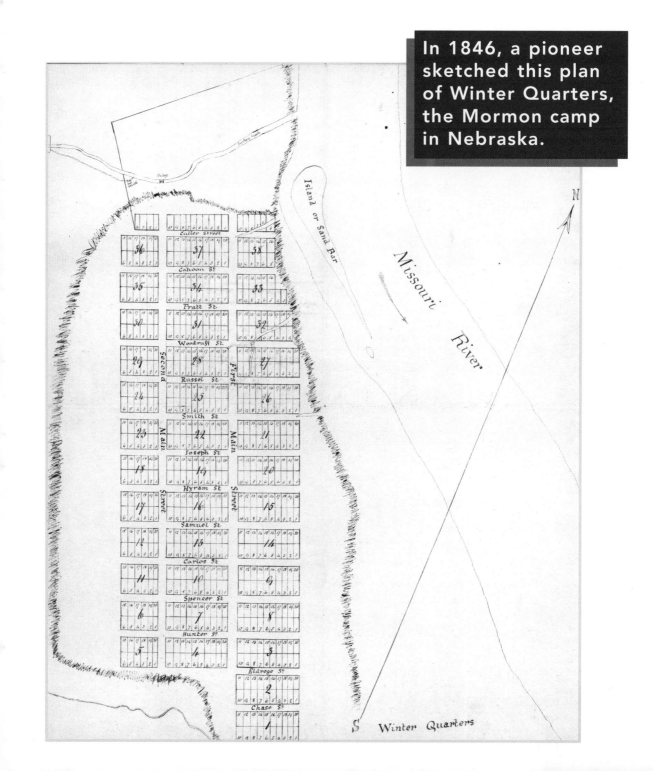

In 1846, a pioneer sketched this plan of Winter Quarters, the Mormon camp in Nebraska.

During the winter of 1846–1847, the Mormon pioneers faced freezing weather, lack of food, and illness. Many did not survive.

Dozens and dozens of camps sprang up as the Mormons prepared to face a cold winter. The settlers were exhausted after traveling hundreds of miles. The **sod** fireplaces they built in their cabins did not provide enough warmth. Food was scarce, and many people became sick.

Out of the nearly 4,000 Mormons at Winter Quarters that season, more than 400 died. Most were very old or very young. That winter is sometimes called the Tragedy of the Winter Quarters.

When spring came in 1847, Brigham Young led a small,

well-equipped company to the Great Salt Lake valley in Utah. The others stayed behind and waited. The moment he saw the area, Young said, "This is the place." This is where they would settle.

As soon as they could, the rest of the Mormons headed for Utah. They had more than 1,000 miles (1,609 km) to go. They still had to cross the Great Plains of Nebraska and Wyoming and the Rocky Mountains.

For the most part, the Mormon pioneers in wagon trains walked to their promised

The Mormon Handcarts

After the first Mormon pioneers went to Utah, thousands more went west each year to join them. Because some pioneers could not afford a covered wagon or oxen, Mormon leaders had simple handcarts built. People walked inside the handle frame to pull the two-wheeled cart. Handcarts carried 100 pounds (45 kilograms) of clothing and bedding, while wagons carried tents, pots, pans, and food.

Pulling a handcart as part of the 150th anniversary celebration of the Mormon trek to Utah land. Some ten years later, those with **handcarts** walked all the way. Even the Mormon families with covered wagons usually walked alongside the wagons. The pioneers had to be careful not to wear out the animals because they would be needed for plowing later. Walking that great distance wasn't easy. As one Mormon said, "My feet were so swollen from walking, I could not wear my shoes."

There were many challenges along the way. The Mormons had to be brave and determined. On the trail, they suffered from blisters, sunburn, broken bones, and snake bites. Mosquitoes, flies, ticks, and lice were also a problem.

Accidents often cost pioneers their lives. During river crossings, wagons sometimes overturned and people drowned. From time to time, a woman's long skirt caught

Mormon pioneers make their way across a river with their wagons and animals.

beneath the wagon's wheels
and pulled the victim under
the oxen's feet or the wheels.

Traveling by wagon could be both dangerous and dull.

Small children who fell were sometimes crushed under the wagon's wheels.

The Mormons had to travel through extreme heat and

pounding rains. Several were hurt or killed by lightning. At times, children were hurt by small windstorms called **whirlwinds.**

But the greatest cause of death on the Mormon Trail was disease. **Cholera,** a disease of the intestines, could quickly spread, with deadly results. It took its toll on the Mormon pioneers heading west. Around one in fifteen died before reaching the Great Salt Lake area.

They were mostly older people and infants.

Life on the trail was an adventure. It was not all hardship. While crossing the plains, the pioneers met and traded with American Indians. The children picked flowers and berries along the Platte River. They also had fun exploring and playing with their dogs at the end of a trail day. The wagon trains usually began and ended the day as a group and with prayers.

This section of today's Platte River is in eastern Wyoming.

Arrival

After Brigham Young and his followers arrived in the Great Salt Lake valley in 1847, they quickly set about building their new home. That place, later known as Salt Lake City, had land for farms. In time, they would build a beautiful temple there.

Salt Lake Temple (top) is built of granite, which workers took from a nearby canyon (bottom) in 1872.

Thousands and thousands of pioneers traveled on the Mormon Trail to reach their promised land.

Over the next twenty years, about 70,000 more Mormons arrived. These pioneers never forgot their journey on the Mormon Trail. They were proud of the sacrifices they made for religious freedom. They passed these feelings on to their children and grandchildren.

Today, Mormons celebrate Pioneer Day on July 24. That was the day the Mormons found their promised land. It was the last stop on the Mormon Trail.

To Find Out More

Here are some additional resources to help you learn more about the Mormon Trail:

Books

Dean, Arlan. **The Mormon Pioneer Trail: From Nauvoo, Illinois to the Great Salt Lake, Utah.** PowerKids Press, 2003.

Erickson, Paul. **Daily Life in a Covered Wagon.** Puffin Books, 1997.

Green, Carl R., and William R. Sanford. **Brigham Young: Pioneer and Mormon Leader.** Enslow Publishers, 1996.

Hester, Sallie. **A Covered Wagon Girl: The Diary of Sallie Hester, 1849–1850.** Blue Earth Books, 2000.

Kalman, Bobbie. **Women of the West.** Crabtree Publishing, 2000.

Kay, Verla. **Covered Wagons, Bumpy Trails.** Putnam, 2000.

Kimball, Violet T. **Stories of Young Pioneers in Their Own Words.** Mountain Press Publishing Co., 2000.

Organizations and Online Sites

Mormon Pioneer National Historic Trail
http://www.nps.gov/mopi/

Visit this National Park Service site to learn more about the Mormon Trail. Be sure to click on the in-depth link for more detailed information about the 1846–1847 trek.

Utah Crossroads
http://www.utahcrossroads.org/

Check out the picture gallery for great color photos of a reenactment of life on the Mormon Trail.

The Pioneer Story
http://www.lds.org/gospellibrary/pioneer/pioneerstory.htm

An interactive Mormon Pioneer Trail map will lead you to pioneer stories on this Church of Jesus Christ of Latter-day Saints site.

Important Words

cholera a serious disease of the intestines

ferries boats that carry people across
a body of water

handcarts small, two-wheeled wagons
pulled by hand

mobs disorderly crowds

pioneers people who explore and settle
an unknown area

promised land a place where one expects
to have a better life; a place that some
believe is promised to them by God

prophet a person whom others believe
speaks for God

sod the top layer of soil from which
grass grows

whirlwinds small spinning windstorms

Index

Meet the Author

Award-winning author Elaine Landau worked as a newspaper reporter, an editor, and a youth-services librarian before becoming a full-time writer. She has written more than 250 nonfiction books for young people, including True Books on dinosaurs, animals, countries, and food. Ms. Landau has a bachelor's degree in English and journalism from New York University as well as a master's degree in library and information science. She lives with her husband and son in Miami, Florida.